real baby animals

goldie the fox

by Gisela Buck and Siegfried Buck

For a free color catalog describing Gareth Stevens Publishing's list of high-quality books and multimedia programs, call 1-800-542-2595 (USA) or 1-800-461-9120 (Canada). Gareth Stevens Publishing's Fax: (414) 225-0377. See our catalog, too, on the World Wide Web: http://gsinc.com

Library of Congress Cataloging-in-Publication Data available upon request from publisher. Fax: (414) 225-0377 for the attention of the Publishing Records Department.

ISBN 0-8368-1506-8

First published in North America in 1997 by
Gareth Stevens Publishing
1555 North RiverCenter Drive, Suite 201
Milwaukee, Wisconsin 53212 USA

This edition first published in 1997 by Gareth Stevens, Inc. Original edition © 1995 by Kinderbuchverlag KBV Luzern, Sauerländer AG, Aarau, Switzerland, under the title *Feha, die kleine Füchsin.* Translated from the German by John E. Hayes. Adapted by Gareth Stevens, Inc. All additional material supplied for this edition © 1997 by Gareth Stevens, Inc.

Photographer: Felix Labhardt
Watercolor artist: Wolfgang Kill
Series editors: Barbara J. Behm and Patricia Lantier-Sampon
Editorial assistants: Diane Laska, Jamie Daniel, and Rita Reitci

Printed in Mexico
1 2 3 4 5 6 7 8 9 01 00 99 98 97

Gareth Stevens Publishing
MILWAUKEE

A mother fox has given birth
to five babies, or cubs.
At first, the cubs cannot see.

One of the cubs is named Goldie.

Goldie nurses, or drinks milk from her

mother's body. But most of the time,

she sleeps.

When the cubs are two weeks old,
they can see. They rub noses with
their mother and explore the den.

During play, Goldie learns what the other cubs are trying to say when they whimper, put their ears back, or show their teeth.

At four weeks old, Goldie explores the world outside the den.

She looks in wonder at everything.

Goldie chases a
butterfly far from
the den. Now she
is lost and afraid.

Goldie's mother
comes to the rescue!
She carries Goldie
back to the den.

At two months old, the
cubs are getting big.

Their mother brings them mice and other
small animals to eat. This will help them
grow bigger and stronger.

The cubs often fight over food.
They soon find out who is the
strongest.

Goldie is old enough now to
hunt on her own. She can
see very well in the dark.

Goldie's baby teeth have fallen out.

She has adult teeth now to help her hunt.

When summer comes, Goldie is ready
to leave her mother's den and live on
her own. Adult foxes live alone.

At the edge of a forest near a stream, Goldie digs her den.

Goldie finds plenty to eat in the shrubs, the forest, and the fields.

One day, Goldie
catches a bird
for dinner.

She also eats
berries and fruit.
Plums are tasty!

Goldie has a thick fur coat
to keep warm in winter.

Catching a mouse in the deep snow
is not easy.   But it's Goldie's lucky day.
She captures her meal.

Males that want to mate
with Goldie fight each other.

The winner of the fight has the honor of mating with Goldie.

After winter is gone, in the month of April, Goldie gives birth to some cubs of her own.

After helping out with the cubs for a few weeks, the father lives on his own.

Goldie has plenty of company in
her den with the newborn cubs.

Further Reading and Videos

Animal Babies in the Wild. (Warner Home Video)
Discovering Foxes. MacQuitty (Franklin Watts)
Fox and Bear. (Beacon Films)
The Fox with Cold Feet. Bill Singer (Gareth Stevens)
Foxes. Lepthien and Kalbacken (Childrens Press)
Foxy Fables. (Hi-Tops Video)
Little Lost Fox Cub. Louis Espinassous (Gareth Stevens)
On the Trail of the Fox. Schnieper (Carolrhoda)
Trill the Fox Cub. Jane Burton (Gareth Stevens)
Watching Foxes. Arnosky (Lothrop)
Wild Fox. A True Story. Mason (Down East)

Fun Facts about Foxes

Did you know . . .

— some varieties of wild foxes are nearly extinct because humans have destroyed their natural habitats?
— there are many folktales and children's stories about clever foxes, in part because foxes are known for being especially skilled in catching their prey?
— foxes come in many colors, such as reddish brown, white, and silver?
— arctic foxes have brown fur in the summer and snowy white fur in the winter?

Glossary-Index

baby teeth — small, weak teeth that many young mammals lose when their permanent, adult teeth grow in (p. 11).

capture — the act of catching by force or cleverness (p. 17).

cubs — the offspring of certain animals, such as foxes and bears (pp. 2, 3, 4, 5, 8, 9, 20, 21, 22).

den — a shelter found or built by an animal in which it can sleep and raise young. A den is usually hidden from view, in a spot that is difficult for other animals to find. This provides a sense of security and safety to the animals living there (pp. 4, 6, 7, 12, 13, 22).

explore — to look around in order to discover what is there (pp. 4, 6).

honor — an award in a contest or competition; the right to a certain thing. Male mammals often fight to determine which one will win the honor of mating with a female (p. 19).

hunt — to search in the wild for animals to capture or kill for food (pp. 10, 11).

mate — when two animals join together for the purpose of producing offspring (pp. 18, 19).

nurse — to drink the milk produced by a female mammal's body (p. 3).

whimper — a noise that an animal makes that is a series of weak, whining sounds. A whimper might mean that the animal is uncomfortable for some reason (p. 5).